MW01142872

Rest on the Flight into Egypt

A.F. MORITZ

Rest on the Flight into Egypt

Brick Books

CANADIAN CATALOGUING IN PUBLICATION DATA

Moritz, A.F.
  Rest on the flight into Egypt

Poems.
ISBN 1-894078-05-5

I. Title.

PS8576.O724R47 1999   C811'.54   C99-931977-9
PR9199.3.M67R47 1999

Copyright © A.F. Moritz, 1999.

We acknowledge the support of the Canada Council
for the Arts for our publishing programme. The support of the
Ontario Arts Council is also gratefully acknowledged.

The cover image is after *Rest on the Flight into Egypt*, c.1518,
by Bernard van Orley (Flemish, 1491/2–1542); reproduction
material, and permission, courtesy of the Art Gallery of Ontario.
The author photo is by Theresa Moritz; protrait by Susana Wald.

Typeset in Trump. Stock is acid-free Zephyr Antique laid.
Printed and bound by The Porcupine's Quill Inc.

Brick Books,
431 Boler Road, Box 20081,
London, Ontario, N6K 4G6

brick.books@sympatico.ca

CONTENTS

Be uprooted and planted in the sea ... afterwards you may eat and drink.

Luke 17: 6, 8

While I was planning my campaign – very carefully, to be invincible, designing the strategy, collecting the overwhelming force – the enemy grew so old that it was shameful to hate him.

Our propaganda, our irresistible self-justification, fell on the whimsy of some old men and many more old women, in that country of widows.

Then we swarmed across the border: bayonets flashed through human suet, grey meat that sagged earthward and slid from the bones of its own accord.

The disease and stink of that country offended our celebrations, but we held them nonetheless, having waited for victory so long.

Now we possessed the field alone, and I went out into the corn, walked and stopped under the gold sky, heard the rattle of my sword and restless clashings of dry stalks.

MANIFESTATION

Antonin Artaud in the middle of the night
last night, like every night, was rooting up
my garden. Breaking off fingernails,
fingertips pouring blood, as if to make a soup
for Don Juan in the tomb, dog-eagerly he scrabbled
in the lilies of the valley. Whenever he found
the rhizomatous root cords he was after,
he'd haul them up, straining his skeleton: I could hear
the vertebrae cracking as his power and the flowers' resistance
bent him double, like the suitors at Ulysses' bow.
Sometimes an arm or hip would pop from its socket
but he scarcely stopped to replace them. He put the roots
over his shoulders, or if one snapped in half
would tie it around his waist or forehead,
fillet of victor or victim, penal or sexual bond,
who knew? He knew. He chewed
the wet mud, broken glass, brick fragments, pennies, old marbles,
centipedes and worms, as he tried to move his face
closer to his goal. The earwigs here for once,
as legend tells, did root in human ears.
The slugs decorated his limestone body with ageless tracts
of shining petroglyphs carved in a single night,
drawing their moist cool trails
medicinally across his anus, distended,
bleeding and on fire with his struggles. As always,
he knew without looking I was there
and said his say: that there's nothing you
(he meant me) don't desire to know but a root
is a root only while it remains underground,
the night troubled to be day turns into day and forgets.
In the morning I found the lilies of the valley
entirely undisturbed, and just beginning to bloom –
a flower I've loved since childhood,
when I would weed around it in my mother's garden

and live the day in its perfume, deep green and white –
and I was relatively content. But this is fiction.
In fact it was late autumn. In the morning I saw the lilies
nothing but brittle, tattered, colourless leaf scaffolding,
and I was relatively filled with hatred
for weather, season, and earth.

Like ghosts leaving their bodies those factories
were leaving us. Their black hulks were lying here,
complex and empty – but we heard that they

were in fact still living, elsewhere. Their souls
had flown to a heaven called Brazil and there
had taken new bodies, glorious, in a new world.

The caged and vented fires there, we heard, the power
of the renovated hammering, the titanic outputs,
the inexhaustible eternity of the materials

and the labour of that world were beyond our imagination,
and the way those mills shone beside plunging rivers
fresher and wider than our oceans here,

the way they stood in the shade of primitive trees and eyes.
And we were shaken by a further rumour: of a flaw
in the world, in being itself, and even deeper –

a flaw in salvation. It was said that those ghosts,
even beatified, were eating heaven – that despite
infinity, they would soon consume it all,

have nothing left, and start on their own bodies.
Was this, then, what awaited us? Not likely. We
were condemned. They sat us down with the manual that said,

'If you are seeking work for fifty hours each week,
then seek for one hundred. Forget sleep. Work
at having no work harder than you ever worked at work:

then you will find work faster and when you find it
you will have learned how to work. Remember,
all who seek will find, and so, think what it means

that you are still seeking. Remember, there's work for all,
but unless you try harder than the others

they will get it and there will be none for you.

Take their work. It will teach them to work better.
You will have what you desire, so think what it means
that you are unemployed and want to die and do not dare.'

I remember that when I wrote this manual we were happy.
It was a difficult, long-drawn-out job,
what with the committee, the management, the board,

and even the shareholders demanding to approve each word,
and in total agreement fighting over the drafts,
differences without distinction, hoping to compose

by mindless opposition something perfectly insipid and bold.
Months, years went by, I was paid well
for my work to be erased, and when we could

we huddled together in the depths of the house.
We had and raised our child, we fought and cried,
watched the birds in the garden at the seed

the manual paid for, though they were free in the wild
to take their glory elsewhere
and find what seed they would.

Then it was all over, the warring factions
were satisfied, the self-help manual
for the unemployed was finished and so was I.

And now that, to help me, they put it in my hand,
I have to contemplate the perfection of my work –
no future book can equal its inescapable clarity –

and its uselessness – neither I nor anyone
will ever find work again. Our child, for instance:
when we were employed we trained him at dire expense

with the greatest artists, and he had already created
his famous series of workers, changed into light and money,
circulating through the elongated noplace

of fibre optics. But now he draws graffiti on walls,
dodging the police, for who can afford canvas?
Or he breaks windows, scrapes stones over marble façades,

writes manifestos on stolen fastfood paper napkins,
identifying himself with the subtle, relentless
markings and destructions of the wind and rain:

for no one is going to buy him any other press
and lithographic stone, no bank is going to invite him
to carve the divine history with all

its demonic grotesques on the new cathedral's door.

To limit yourself to what can be said abundantly
would be a science like that of what can be known,
or the other of what can be done: a lazy science.

A joyful science of the joy of limits. That is
a tragedy, and anyone around here can watch scientists
enjoying the tragedium of a wet grey Sunday

all he wants already. But what can be said barely
nursed through the nigged nipple of impossibility ...
now, there is richness for the hankering baby's cry.

The abundance of the scientists of abundance
is balanced by the oblivion of the singer of want
as deprivation balances the baby Fat:

somewhere to go for someone who has grown
to squeeze out all the milk and marrow of a world
and drain it flat and fill it up from end

to end. Somewhere not easy to find: no forest
up Rio Perososo in the noonday sun
where discoveries find themselves and natives die

of love for the victor and conquistadors
in crowds watch, rippling their toes on chaises longues
and applauding. Somewhere, in less timely happier climes,

where snow falls, wind blows, and no one knows,
invention is difficult, the material being, and
the tool, return to a depopulated native land of ice.

The philosophers are examining this man
who seems to be sleeping. To palpate
his soft tissues they have to kneel

around the old scratched walnut bed, hands in the tatters
of the tattersall, and to keep from waking
the subject they have to whisper – so low

that from a slight distance their words all sound like God
bless mummy and daddy ... Now it's midnight,
two hours into the fearful experiment:

banyans, grasses like rock crystal sabres, spider plants
two hundred feet high have marched through the titanium doors
and grown over him. The boots of the learned

ur-theologians are filled up with scorpions.
The cure for malaria has been undiscovered
and those of them who have not died are drinking quinine,

shivering on a crumbled verandah. They trade
badinage with a consumptive young prostitute,
her song of hope wasted is far better than hope,

and they keep their minds on their work.
Now it's four a.m. and the subject has fallen
into a well. Nothing any more exists around him,

even his bed and his tormentors are gone
and he tumbles endlessly in wellness.
This is pictured by the instruments and the doctors watch it:

an image enhancement, that shows what it looks like
to live in utter darkness and be too small to be seen,
'looks like' here having to be taken in a special sense

that corresponds only analogically to 'looks like.'
So for the hour between four and five

it seems he is splashing down and down through strata

of water or fire: something that wavers as he hits,
resists and then admits him, shimmering
in concentric rings of light that still and still

as he descends, floating, falling and drowning beneath,
until he strikes the next level, and the whole
drama of impact and absorption repeats.

And is this anything but words? The computer model
struggles to feel its digits, and now outside
the birds are waking up, if they ever slept,

if they aren't just an unresting system
that tortures itself with lack of rest
but fortunately it can't feel, or the broken egg

fallen on the ground before it could hatch
is symbol and reality of one,
one at least, who has rested.

The thieving light glimmers and puts back exactly
in place what it took when it left: the dresser
with its streaked three-leaf mirror is ready

to reflect a face that lives or dies
of being here, and is yet not here.
And now he's awake. He hears birds, and there are birds.

And now he lifts his head.

They're on a train marooned in the central desert:
the tracks have turned to rust and blown away.
No path at all remains now through the blue sand,
and no animal has passed, no weed has nodded here
since three a.m., when the last moisture
was sucked up by the moon.

Heirs to a billion years of desiccation,
they called for an atmosphere of fire. Now cry
and the tears hiss and vanish,
and lightning in that mist at times lights up
a half-demolished house – its shattered walls
show fallen plaster, shameful boards,
wallpaper stained with wine, and the astronomer
at his desk in the sleet
erases his numbers again.

Here in the train the bar car is exhausted
and they play pharaoh as dunes creep up the windows.
The waves of earth are closing, someone says,
over our heads – that, or we're filtering down
to the bottom of an undug well,
and one day a man with a rod will signal us
from above, tapping too desperately on the rock.

SCIENCE

Knowing that girls once went naked under slender palms
didn't end my desire for these women
in mud-and-sweat-caked nylons.

And understanding that everyone closes the door, the mouth,
and does just what I do in silence –
this only left me more secret in myself.

I learned our open ways contradict the cruel past
yet felt I was rightly condemned,
chained in a black cell, in a castle founded on injustice.

And the discovery I'm like all others, am nothing but others,
is what hardened the darkness close around me
and made me keep alone.

A sparrow passing through in fall
came to my tree to look
for the bird-feeder I once had
but now have taken down.

A neighbour feared the birds it brought,
a divorcee, who said
her father had raised pigeons and
had thrown them at her head

when she was small and he was mad –
so now, she said, she had
a phobia about all birds:
would we stop feeding them?

I was translating, at that time,
a work of genius on
fiery woman, sexual god,
from Spanish, from a man.

And how to reconcile with his
mad love the careful anguish
she, brittle goddess, felt? – which now
my period shall extinguish.

I watched the disappointed bird
turn on the branch and gaze
from every angle possible
on the new-empty space,

and saw that if I just stood up
and took him in my hand,
he would consent to be comforted
and learn to understand.

But then the vision passed. Again
it was obvious if I
made any movement fear would make
the baffled sparrow fly.

DISCOVERY

A site that might have been a temple or an igneous intrusion.

Signs of ancient fire. No footprints

in the yellow hardened ground, unless those scars are footprints.

Calling out, you think you've been here before: the cliff

returns your voice.

Examining, you think you know what the letters mean.

If in fact you have received any letters.

If these are letters and not accidental scratches in the rock.

The wind dies down. Full of desire,

you want to bow your head. It stays erect and staring.

These tumbled pillars might be ribs of the earth.

These crosses might be minerals or shadows.

The one certain sign of submission is death.

The only silence is silence.

Your compass and your clock have the same face

as this shattered undulation of poor land.

The disused road cut through rock and an eroding wind

bare something buried,

your second self, among these hills.

A man sits down quietly, holding his head in his hands.
The face is facing him,
and it looks into his eyes.

The two of them are not anxious to speak.
Slowly all comes clear
because their gaze is so completely clear.

And each time that it penetrates farther into the skull,
picking out the true form and all the colours
of something that had always been dark,

one of them says a single sentence
and the other one answers. Thus knowledge advances,
and the man advances through the world to the very end.

But this is wrong. The man has only one
face, one voice, one look that is pushed around by the wind.
He doesn't see himself clearly,

doesn't know what he looks like to another,
even his body is vague to him,
and he feels that he goes on talking and talking,

or singing, returning a little more worn out
to the same words, as they say a lost man always
comes across his own steps, circling in the desert.

THE LITTLE WALLS BEFORE CHINA

A courtier speaks to Ch'in Shih-huang-ti, ca. 210 B.C.

Highness, the former walls were helpless. They
stood alone in the middle of small fields
protecting nothing. A single peasant's holding
engulfed each one as it ran briefly, straight
from noplace off to noplace, with ruinous steps
of broken stone at both ends. Only head-high,
without the towers, gates and towns of your great wall,
they stuck where they were, never rising over hills
or curving through valleys: nothing but shoddy masonry
and a mystery: who built them, how long ago,
what for? They seemed to have no role but balking
the reaper and the ox; their bases made
islands in the flashing scythe-strokes, where wild flowers
and shrubs sprouted.

           So all the people praise you
for burying such walls and their memory
in your vast one, which joins them, stretching far
beyond where they once crumbled to hold your Empire:
a wall which therefore can never have an end
but has to go on extending itself forever.
How useful, how cogent your wall is: a pale
for the civilized, a dike against the wild people
outside, who trade their quiet human blood
for the rage of gods, tearing men to pieces,
throwing them, watching them fall. In burying
those little walls, Lord, you have covered our shame
at our ancestors, best forgotten, whose mighty works
were so pointless, or so pitiably useless.
Was all their effort so that daisies could grow in fissures?
So that some human work would rise over the flats
and weather till it seemed not human? Only
so that something of ours could be like trees and rocks:
docile-seeming, yet sullenly opposed
to use, and when compelled, only half serving,
reserving from the functions that we give them

a secret and idle self. The peasants would make
lean-tos for cattle against those walls: they served
for this alone.

Now scholars, Lord, are saying
the gods are not bulls and cows. That in ancient times
we herded these animals to keep from starving
and going naked, and so came the old custom
of thinking them gods – from dependence. In my youth,
I know, the peasants said just the opposite.
Worship came first. The awesome bull and cow
were gathered to be adored more easily,
till people noticed how they let themselves
be driven and penned. Next came the first murders
against these gods, and the careful observation
that they stood to be killed. And so their cult became
contempt of beings that would live with us
and submit to our crimes and hunger, and we began
to breed them. That is why, the farmer says,
cattle are honoured, murdered, eaten, cherished
with labour that makes him their slave, and that is why
in summer he exults in blood, but shivers with fear,
with exhausted terror and regret, and sinks into
stunned revelry all winter, eating the salted meat,
getting children, his house closed up with snow,
himself awake as if he slept, living
as if he had already died, and rich, happy
as if he were a buried worm.

Is God,
then, Highness, the fat flaccidity of cattle?
Myself, I don't like to wonder anymore.
I only hope lifelong service earns what I ask:
the command of some far bastion on your wall
where it curves out into the unsettled wastes
beyond any field, and the barrenness inside
is indistinguishable from that without.
This is the reward and end of life I want:

to be a point, though infinitely small
and far from you, in that wide circle centred
on your great self. I see myself arriving
to take charge of my troops. I look down from the tower:
bare plains, outcrops of ice and rock, vast restless
stirrings of grey grasses and dark-veined overcast,
the cold wind's hissing. Year after year the same,
waiting for an assault that never comes,
straining to glimpse our naked enemies
creeping blended with their stony soil: nothing
but legend, it may be. Maybe a morning
will rise when, waking, I find that I've forgotten
which way is north, and can't tell if I am turned
outward to danger or inward, Highness, to you.
The sun invisible, a murky light diffused
throughout featureless cloud, and the wall so long
no curve appears – it seems to stretch out straight
endlessly east and west: what clue will there be
which way to face my people for the attack?
It will be crucial then to show no doubt.
My orders, I vow, though ignorant, will be crisp.

A winged bull, vast, overshadowing a gate,
a megalith of empty blackness opening on a city's crumbs,
a plain of bricks halved and halved again.
Wings, clouds flickering in the sky: as if gods are burning
huge birds alive up there, and the smoke and ashes
turn to still vaster, darker curved soft breasts and wings,
the sooty feathers rise and fall, cover earth and heaven,
till even the orange-blue streams of flame high overhead
vanish, and the low expanses of rubble sink in soot.
A bull, too large, wings, a human face, all much too large;
the wild fever for images of more than man
joined these together here, having torn each piece
from its own place, though each remained where it was,
untouched, unmoved. For you still hear the eagle's wing,
the owl's, the buzzard's, rush past you in the dark.
The ox, ploughing on the hill's rim against lead-coloured dusk,
is still where it was, a beast of God. And your own face,
small, soft on its crude bone: it masks you still –
you retrace it there and cover it with your hands.

You burnt my father's house, lord,
and you were kind to him,
you killed him. My mother
and sisters you left there wailing,
hurting themselves against charred blocks,
digging in their naked breasts with
onyx combs. Looking back, I saw them
envying me as you drove me
bleeding across the rubble: wolves
down from the mountains, ground-breaking frosts
and all the pools diseased
shone in their eyes.

In your own palace you threw me in a dark room,
a filthy barrack, to be kicked
and spit on by your countrywomen, desperate
at still one more foreigner brought
to devour the grace they waited for.
Rarely did you visit me, briefly,
and bare the bloated, gnarled
sex that hung there dead
on your vanquishing thighs.
And if I could not raise it, you beat me
till I could not rise. I thought then
of the boys of my own land, fighting
or riding naked, the wind
and the sight of our eyes holding them,
slender eagerness they could not hide,
power as of mountain brooks, the male sex of my
people, erased – slaughtered
by you, lord. Sometimes this
excited me, and so helped me.

And now that in a few years
the light will be sinking from the surface
of my face and body, as in mid-summer
water would sink and hide deep in the marrow
of my desert land, you've sold your servant –

sold me to ones who never would have bought
except for their terror of you.
I have to leave you and go to my third house,
third prison, the coldest,
and I have to see my life:
a path of sharp flints winding down
to a wind-pierced hovel, and from its door
a path to a roofless hovel
lower still. I howled out
that I love you, my fingers tried to clutch
the ice-like marble, I tore my dress
so the breasts, wet with blood, would cling
to the stone as they dragged me.

Now I dream of you with longing.
How old, weak you are,
how the unfallen city that you rule
falls away from you.
I dream that you come to me again
in need, crusted in blood, dust, your own
filth, but in my mouth I take your lips,
I take your eyes, fingers, sex,
I clean and comfort all
your body, lumpish and swollen,
defeated, with my small mouth.

I called this love and you laughed,
you called it fear. But it's not
for you, lord, except as you are
a part of everything that falls to me.

When the gods begin to create,
their fingers, speed and death,
separate and mix pure masses:
light and air,
minerals and the sea.
Abundance:
why should anything last?
And making and remaking
never
do they ask themselves
will these things come again,
will this day's exact joy
recompose itself,
or is there only so much time:
not enough
for the wheel to return ever
to just this point?

The visibly lengthening track
of a crab too small to be seen
across the rose and gold
wet beach at dusk,
when each pebble throws its own
infinite shadow up the sand,
the sun is so low on the ocean ...
of this great work being
lost or destroyed, this evening,
we love most of all
a section of background
in the far left, high up,
hanging in air:
an arch as of purple granite
and beyond it nameless colours,
distilled
in a region where no bodies are
and colour floats alone.

Who cares now

to return to the source,
where the gods' fingers first touch matter?
Better to stay
in this late splendour,
perpetual revolution
of daily wonder, the broken
columns wearing away
to new visages
in the day passing over
and the wind,
random sculptor. Clouds,
ancient monuments – all
are lost, lost again and found
unchanged. Or remade,
and memory is too weak to know
these discoveries of ours
are old things freshly
come to light, the same
that rain once washed away
and earthquake buried.

Here by the southern ocean
spring
while in our Ontario
October reigns,
wind passing through goldenrod
and tall grass on a hill,
torpid wasps in the pine needles,
dragonflies, the air warm,
with a forecast of cold
that draws in the stream
clear outlines of first red
leaves that float down: things
flowing through a world far away
in wavering forms that are
our bodies
while here now dusk
and the Pacific are our thought.

EGG NOODLES

We are on our way to the Generalissimo Nguyen Van Thieu,
the cheapest restaurant in town, she says, but good,
where a family of four (drinking water) can eat
for twelve ninety-five. Despite the name,
it turns out the Thieu is a Chinese restaurant run
by a Japanese family – a fact that can be explained
by various changes of ownership, but I won't try.
We go in and order a couple of piles of entropy.
Preserving the time-honoured fare, the Japanese
have nevertheless introduced certain innovations:
in the soup, for instance, each egg noodle
is equipped with its own miniaturized television.
Goodness gracious we say though gracious isn't the word
but the traditional tea ceremony at dinner's end
makes up for this. More than makes up. Because to prove
that modern technology is not at odds with spirit,
the owners have invested this ritual
with a meditative prolongation and subtlety
unimaginable to the ancient Japanese.
First the tea is brewed, and we contemplate the brewing,
our breathing slows, eighty years pass, our blood
has turned to dust and our bodies withered
like January apples, until they also sift away
while the tea is served, we scatter on its non-existent
currents as the steam drifts up, and swirl motionlessly.
By then there is no one else left in the place
but staff: we can see the cook behind the curtain
in the tiny kitchen making his preparations for next day,
installing televisions in the noodles of tomorrow's soup.

TO HIS COY MISTRESS

Your pleasures are immediate,
curled in themselves like any cat,
while the great truck wheels going by
outside our curtains make me cry.
Why am I thus so much dismayed
by transience? Our rent is paid
and I am even at times employed:
we can afford my cult of void
and dreaming it alive with forms –
bodies – as if angelic swarms
of bees, now homeless, yet alive,
blocked out all vision of their hive
burning to less than a memory,
a ruin where the root should be.

Nothing if not intransient,
insisting on what time has meant
by its blank hours, too short and long,
worth song, worth no more than a song,
I have rhymed out the sermon of
desperate sex, the love of love,
to you, the way a priest will rave
at all the absent, while the nave
redoubles his anger on the few
who are there, shifting in a pew
and dozing, warm in their own breath,
content in disregarded faith,
half-watching light-rafts dawn has thrown
through dusty windows cross dark stone.

ON FARMING

Speaking seriously now
of how you live, expired,
the words are the ways. Your ticket
was for the passage, so you thought,
but the packet came undone
and a bunch of things not unlike birds
arose and dispersed
in metallic heaven. No white concern sails
the waterway anymore, its huge
lily pads come and knock on the door
with telegrams relating the malevolent intent
of in-laws armed from beyond the borders.
It's safer to stay home. The automobile storm
mounts in fury and now and again
is parted from zenith to horizon
by depression and a delayed clap of unemployment.

Your album tells you of the mirrors
of days into which you fitted
like something missing.
Now there's too much time
to think of friends as part of you,
to absorb the bland weather in the coruscating
peace of your thoughts. All is idleness.
With the excitement of one who has spilled the marbles,
you gaze through the endless caucus
at the threshing floor and spin
on the mystery's point: how reassemble
the unreaped from this strenuous dust.

It's hot but it's almost November,
one bee left in wilted white and red
impatiens, and a wood thrush
dead against the glass wall-door between
kitchen and garden:

the head bent back, the feathers cool and eyes
congealed, the body tossed in covering tones
of the leaf ruins blown and caught
in the same corner. On the wood

wall above the bed
of linen and haemorrhage coloured flowers, the wild
grapes are gone, finished by passing birds,
and the great tangled vine that was a ladder
to the higher air – crowded with flies once,
with wasps, bees, ants and ladybugs moving all
directions up and down, humming, conflicting –

is quiet, not one passenger. Now another
wood thrush lights on a branch and looks
and looks, flies off, comes back, looks,
and looks. And there is your word only,

human, watching, for the tender
evil dream that now in the living bird the spouse
goes fading down, back, in the dark
brain alone.

I'm sitting here as if studying the dust
but it's a postcard reproduction in my palm:
Bernard van Orley's 'Rest on the Flight into Egypt,'
which is the great painting in that same order
where ' ''Twas on a Holy Thursday' is the great song.

Earth's perfected beauty, the city that could be,
tall mountains, blue distance and feminine river
signalling that God will let us stay here a long time,
in this place we loved at first sight, though it is ordained
that some day we'll have to leave: all this
is open in my hand. All this is in the picture
because of the mother and sleeping child,
who need a world to be in. And so there is Joseph,
the grizzled calm old guardian who sees clearly
how helpless he'd be to defend them. So too
the donkey with bright carnelian saddle cloth
and olive-coloured water gourds, feeling itself
loved for its service and nature. Van Orley has shown things
as they are: no hidden interiors
that need a key or principle lost with the Chaldeans
to open, but daylight
on white water, golden cinq-foil, spectral paints.

Life is better now than ever before. Short decades ago
neither this postcard nor any colour reproduction
could have been printed. And to have a small replica
of the dead man's painting makes nonsense of the old days,
when you had to sit alone in the ragged virgin land
with nothing, constructing your own pleasures:
maybe a jerry-built unpainted porch over a valley.
You used to be left either to fail in your own
imagining, or to glory in its power as you made up
some spot of peace between the draining memories
of green Egypt and the frothing Holy Land.
Better not to be alone but have this reproduction,
as you sit in the weedy scrub, moved to blankness
by the grandeur of antique fragments: the breached

beehive kilns and walls of the dead firebrick works.
Better not to be isolated on this hard, used ground
among baked weeds and flying grasshoppers,
black, green and gold, where the creek flows
past houses without doors and trees veiled
in tent-worm and wild grape and honeysuckle vines.
Better to have with you this copy of van Orley's work
prepared by a huge press that properly
registers every colour, to be faithful, perfectly.

In the doorless doorways the doors are the black
coffin-shapes of darkness within. Life's better now.
Surgery, for instance, is no longer to saw the limb
without anaesthetic. And if some doctor's anaesthetic
conversation spoils it a little, it remains a truer worship
than the praying of lice-ridden crowds that scourged themselves
to halt a plague. New technologies have removed
the need for firebricks, and the steel mills
have been exported to lands where workers still work
long and cheap, lands that enjoy more than we do,
with a more youthful fervour, pouring acids into streams.
Living fossil lands, they show how things used to be
here, when in these ruined shells of mills
workers, like the flesh in crabs, still quivered.

Food's always on the table here, for most,
and isn't that the ancient sign – plenty – that proves
a people and a prophet chosen? The multitude
is fed. In the old days, the crowd
would go out into the desert and behold a story
copied from an older story, of loaves endlessly multiplied,
and not be fed: everyone heard
until he was not satisfied
and at the end nothing was left over.
Yet some, strong or lucky to have a place near the front
with a good view, did come away inspired,
though others fainted or grew bored
at the back of the massed people where they played cards

with the diseased and unemployed
and never saw the speaker or knew what the assembly
was all about, why they had trailed out so far
with all the rest to the pink, howling rocks,
why they trailed back later
to their blazing streets. Each part of that crowd
has its descendants to this day, and they fight
for possession of the electromagnetic waves.

But how far I've come trudging the paradisal roads
of this minuscule copy of 'Rest
on the Flight into Egypt' – far,
and all in the wrong direction,
toward a personal and unmeaning bitterness.
In me is the radiance of sun on a clay jug,
a leather saddle strap, the ladybug climbing my wrist,
while the understanding mocks every contentment,
every human thought. Yet all things here
are marvels: a little farther on
is a knoll where the white sun's setting disk overflows
through feathery olive trees, arresting
vision, since they do not grow in this land.

Bronze pages scattered on the open ground.
No shadow of a house. No plan,
no picture scratched on a broken tile.
No voice can give the agitation of wind
honed where it moves nothing,
its whirling blade and metal
howling, and the sparks.

What do I remember? A city
in these mountains erased, a tree
by a brick wall, and in its needles
sometimes sparrows, planets, angels, bells, lights.
In the shadow of the house, the family lived.
The piano exulted and moaned over the wind.
Bronze leaves, green needles
glowed through the black walls
and were with them in the room –
just as the great forest, the star-wood, burns again
on earth when finally night comes.

Nothing happened here – nothing ever
happened in our city, and yet it was destroyed.
What could the innocent citizens have done?
Heirs to two hundred years of despising whoever wished them well,
it had become part of their blood: they could not know
that they were proud and dark and suicidal,
that they had grown content to let their own
houses – with these building paper fronts and grey windows,
wedding receptions on the gravel driveways
and burnt lawns – sink back into
a dusk and trash and landscape God.

                                      Unshaven,
halfway along to work with his rusted black lunch pail,
passing the dusty trees-of-heaven, blinded
by morning sun on concrete walls of the underpass,
on the road to Gate No. 9, the 16-inch rolling mill,
he told me once: 'No human wisdom can build a city
and confer a way to live. Or if it does,
if it was the dead who passed down these flaming tracks,
this schedule of peace and steel that evolves more slowly
than the sun bloodies its hands upward and the species undress,
then it's only because time uses humans the way a flood
sweeps everything down and along,
making it rot, and later spreads some of it on the seeds.'

So going around the city while it still struggled
like a beetle half-smashed, I saw
some places that answered to the Louvre,
palaces but built by a feeble, violent desire.
Four white marble urns atop the flat façade
of the long-abandoned discount furniture store.
A stone balustrade before a vista of graceful trees
riven by reflecting water clear to the setting sun,
and in a room behind, redoubled
on a closed piano lid, a painting by Asher Durand
of this same view, though he had never seen it.

And everywhere, strange mutations in the slow
but visible decline. The animals we knew in childhood
were all gone now, and nothing survived
larger than a china figurine on a lamp table:
pigeons and mourning doves with asbestos beaks,
sparrows of creosote that slung their chirps like stones.
At dawn and dusk staggering squads of boys
hunted incompetently for rabid, thieving skunks and squirrels,
beat up young husbands, slashed mothers, took
what they wanted, what was there.

                          The river
is quiet now. Ducks have returned. Remember
how we once saw it, in the steady roar and rhythmic
pounding of the mills, changed to a silver pudding
by some powerful process by now long bankrupt and gone?
It looked like melting aluminum, or the grey slurry
that falls from a milkshake machine on humid nights
when the button is punched. What did they ever do here
but buy what was put before them at the prices marked?
The great seven-story central tower, all cream-white tile,
of the closed dairy factory stands there, set
into the wooded cliff, and two Gothic dwarves
above its boarded entrance
still bear up the beautiful wall on their crushed backs.

I want to write a book of chaste and simple verse
harmonious with the calm regard of this bare room,
high up and poor, whose grimy window looks across
the forest of the rooftops, a black continent,
to the moon rising and the smoke it colours white
in a sky of darkening ink. But thunder crumbles calm,
and the storm is translated to the centre of this room.
The fiery crystal drops fall pure from boiling clouds
on the shingles; then here inside the falling is repeated
in a new form: fragments of plaster shaken down
by the rain patter on the desk, and rusty water starts
to plink in cans and streak the walls.

                                 So by the law
of ambivalence the water of purification contains
the filth of the roads: and this is all the astrologer
discovered, ages ago, when he lived in this same attic,
and stared across the great unpopulated city
of roof tiles, chimney pots, stone gables, leaning brick
smokestacks, the mists of dying skies and furnaces –
his empire, the high crossings, where his eyes walked alone
or sometimes with a bird or thought for a companion.

Not even you, dead peaks, are my discovery:
for every renter of this room already knew you.
Not even the utter deadness of the sun's glory rising
over your burning pitch, its brilliance and shadows engraved
in pain that slowly does pass. Not even, more alive,
the storm's random fury when it tears at you, and the wind,
probing to enter your slate body, makes it writhe,
rips pieces from it, throws them down on the back alleys,
finds no way in, withdraws, subsides to a tender dripping.

And it's like that now. Now it's night and storm and nothing
is to be seen out there but lightning in black panes
stuttering almost ceaselessly, and in its rare pauses

the reflection of my lamp and the room hung in the night:
this room, poor, bare and small, up near the sky, deafened
by the barrage of thunder, where my listening goes on
for indistinguishable howlings masked by wind and rain,
as if a mob, a shattered army, copulated
in black mire, the oil of swamps, its own blood, in its sleep.

RESCUE

With breasts like footballs embedded in their chests
and covered with skin that seems just like the stuff
commercial photographers use to make those sundaes
that last unmelting through a long shoot under hot lamps,
came the not-quite-women who were not quite men.

I was channel surfing but I slipped from my board,
the undertow dragged me down, I struck my head on a soft
rock, and these are the mermaids that came to save me,
take me to their grotto, and I have to marry them
or drown, have to give them a child but they have no womb.

I remembered then a sudden jolt that once slammed shut
the door of a barley-dusty boxcar, trapping me somewhere
in a marshalling yard outside of Pittsburgh. I lay
with my apple jack and dreamed – this was 1967 –
the hippies would save me if only they knew I was there.

Sometimes I screamed a little and scrabbled at the latchless
inside of the door in the complete darkness, or dreamed
the skeletal yellow mummy I would be, its smile
lighting up to welcome the discoverers, months in the future,
when they came to clean out and use that car again.

At dawn the door shrieked, a square of blinding light
opened in blackness, and gradually from it stood forth
four railroad dicks with drawn guns, expecting who knows what
malevolent tramp, what demon against which maybe
a gun would be no use. So of course they laughed at me.

They wanted to turn me in to my mother to save me
and so demanded my name. Shaking, gulping the clear wind
too violently even to lie, I gave it. They wouldn't believe.
So I made up a false one and they let me go back to my ditch
to hide and watch for another train slowly picking up speed.

DISAPPOINTMENT

Inward mask that stares. Flat hammered disc,
crude bronze beaten and gouged the shape and size
of human faces. Circle that turns in space,
identical on both sides, and through the gaps
of mouth- and eye-holes, and around the rim,

vision circulates: dusk, night-blue slag,
orange and gold fire falling from clouds
that cool and harden over a river valley.
Grey river flecked with white. Its empty bridge.
Its city made from fragments of black rock

cut into softened domes, false pyramids
and leaning chimneys worn smooth, slender and light
by the wind. A star leaps from floating metals
and you will soon be sleeping. Savour it:
peace lit by shouts, clangings, an echoed wail,

peace to be drowned in new awakings. A cold child
will rip worn night with his nail, and a rusted
hinge, an iron bird, will be singing. But now
through black and white lights, under sealed windows,
in your sleep along the rainy wall peace walks.

Hard to recapture now how wonderfully free
I felt in this old world when it was still the new.
Our age dawned first as perfect loss: one day I woke
and guilt was gone. The problem of evil suddenly

was left alone – it bored everyone – and so it attacked
with new viciousness: the dragon of romance became
a dinosaur. It kidnapped woman. I grabbed my spear
to seek them in the endless forest, hew down their covert,

slaughter him, marry her, and hear again
through starlight at play on her shadowed navel the faint roaring,
the faint rustling, the infinite night disclosing
the murmur of the next still undiscovered people.

Even to remember how nakedness, new, rare, and briefly flashing,
compensated for the torture of the single endless
sunset that disappoints all mornings
is hard, now that the nude is everywhere,

long established, not evil, not guilty, not hungry
in this post-modest clarity where all that counts
is family and loyalty, work and longevity.
City, forest, wood of women, and the world wars:

hitting the beaches full of blood, mounting desire, and confidence
that our godlike enemies were like ourselves but worse,
laying down our fire to an algebraic pattern
good anywhere, even in the abstract vacuum ...

it is all gone now, swallowed in its own perfection.
Tonight I went out on one of those long solitary
rambles through the redounding metropole, one of those aimless
reveries by which I first built, in the old days,

all that nature has commanded us to build.
Bypassing the knifings, rapes, and more insouciant injustices,
I prayed to her inwardly: to nature, our mother

and lover, in whom accomplishment

and impatience are one, who creates and sharpens desire
with the impossibility of fulfilment,
the derisive dream she gave us that some day we,
lice on her body, would hold her face to face.

For once my prayer was heard: I saw that the times
were completed. There was no nature anymore, only a few
specimens of what had been: preserved with care,
placed lovingly in corners, as though she were

in these scraps. Earth was a zoo in a park,
and the fate of species, my old adversaries, hung on my whim
and my funding decisions. I was boss, who had thought myself
only the flower in tall grass, the gnat on the gnu.

I recall that as I walked and wondered, the paved way fell
into a gentle bushy decline, and for a moment
enringed by green I almost felt that nature
had come again, for in the leaves I lost sight

momentarily of every sign. But quickly the path
rose back up as planned and I could see there were people
everywhere, I saw nothing but people.
But I was gone.
What came up out of that slight depression was you.

A block, a block, a block ... and then
a man, leaned by a doorway with
the fated precision of a clock
long dead. Then block, block, block, then man.

Remember all you can, do all
you can to call back something else,
not this same sequence that extends
like wallpaper figures in a house:

a mean house that the wrecker tore
one side from and let stand, to show
the dreary halls and rooms inside:
perfect reflections of the streets.

The green paint of the rotted joists
sweats, and you let your head rest there,
take comfort. And yet love was not,
once, the loud ticking of your feet

in silent night past bricked-up stations,
was not this taste for vacant lots,
lanes scrawled and littered, mills torn down,
the city dead but for you alone.

THE SPECIALISTS

Not much longer will anyone still live here,
in this city our words so richly fail to capture.
Yet here is life – the only life, that feeds
on all the others. Here alone is Justice,
from some deep distance come, features much worn down,
and sweet animals still awhile under her rich trees
glimpsed as they go away, fells rippling
on lithe haunches swallowed in the leaf smoke.

Justification of many an unjust pain
drives them. They will be gone, but we remain
as a nurse watches the hour and the sweating head.

Already now it's the age of specialists:
flesh, grass, and rock each has its own,
proclaiming loves and wars to raze this world
and raise the true one from its shards and seeds.
But we stay by our ancient Justice flecked with blood
in the centre of her city. And while they are green,
we still circulate singing in the parks
that grew around her. Hers is the only beauty.
Disconsolately let us fail one final time,
the most difficult, pure failure, to capture it,
talking of her decrees, and the hue and twist
of leaf and beast falling.

THE DOOR

All day the day had hardened, narrowing in
with the anger of a wall as it is made
to be perfect, higher, and the last gaps closed:
a day tightening self-annoyance over the skin,
with noises of clashed metals filling thought.

Then, night, how you opened it. You let
a first planet be glimpsed as through the black narrow ray
of a door drifting open on dark.
It slowly swung so wide,
the whole field beyond the sill imperceptibly came in,
and the room was now worlds shining
down to the far edges of a clearing
and hung in sprays in the wood.

Later – before dawn – I stepped outside
and saw the sun's slow light
erase the weightless stillness … watched
hungrily, tired of waiting,
as night's old freedom now was cancelled again.
I saw the skies above the sky be locked away
beyond new distances that rose,
lesser but more bright – saw the door close
and it again be day.

THAT DAY

I won't be able to tell you about that day
because though the sun rose, I'd forgotten the word sun,
and birds sang but I'd forgotten those two words,

which I know now and remember having known before.
But that day when I woke I didn't know it was 'waking'
or what had been 'asleep.' I walked in the garden,

the gently twisted path to every vista – tangled
remnants of forest, smooth shining water in a low valley,
the terrace of naked statues: divine wind-scarred

adolescent flesh ... I walked in the garden as if
in a camp of cardboard huts on the tenth day of rain,
and in the dark green shade on the blue shore

by yellow iris blossoms (I had forgotten those words
and it flashed across imagination, in place of memory,
that our cold maids call them 'boxes of the dawn') ...

I walked in the garden: and my soft breath was the cough
of someone dying, lungs filled with salt and blood
that never again can reach the penetrating air.

The leaves on spring-dark boughs were far away
as winter. I sat and held a crystal cube
and turned it in my lap, and worldless,

in a cold wind and a space that were not even
wind or space, I scrabbled at my crystal
with twiglike fingers and could not get in.

What I had was nothing, as the poor say, 'We have nothing.'
But there was only a gape there, like no mouth
groping to talk, to taste. No nothing. No more.

THE UNDERTAKER

Necesitas comer, pero, me digo,
no tengas pena, que no es de pobres
la pena, el sollozar junto a su tumba ...
– Vallejo

Since they all have their undertakings, why
is it I alone who have to talk too softly,
keep too clean, drink, despise myself, in this
mansion I've preserved? They would have torn it down
and forgotten the old judge who lived here. My father
buried him, and hundreds, and I buried hundreds
till I could buy this place. So now I sit here
some afternoons, in the lulls that do occur
in dyings as in traffic: an empty house
with seven living rooms and not one kitchen,
with four dozen velveteen divans and armchairs
occupying the walls, with empty vases
always at ready and a smell of sachets and tissue.
Or I straighten up my work tables in the basement
in the room next to the furnace.

                    Someone contracts
to manage the corpse of whatever it was ... the soul,
the life, the one ... that's gone. Someone contracts
to carry that dead weight, clean away that leaving,
that dropping – so that those who used to love it
can weep unashamed, unencumbered, unrestrained.
The freedom and cleanliness of their grief: no lingering
with the heavy meat, the garbage, the clumsy
shamelessness of the dead, dripping, lolling, stinking,
open-mouthed, legs splayed thoughtlessly, the idiot
postures and expressions, the newborn helplessness.
The corpse is given to me the way an infant
is given to a nurse, or a fouled room
to a housemaid. My grandmother, when she came
in the mornings to this famous house to scour
the huge black cast-iron ovens, must have looked
at its gables and woven arbours sparkling among leaves

as I look at these mourners, aristocrats of loss.

Maybe it's right they call their squealing and gossip
mourning: a pun for daybreak, when confusion comes.
At dawn you swear to remember the fading night's
glimpsed exaltations but forget that promise
in the new sunlight or dead overcast, the grating,
which absorbs you until you are perfectly content,
of the day's business. In neighbouring rooms
I once laid out Mrs. Harris, the senile teacher
(I remember her rambling endlessly about
the forest clearings, the clay-floor cabins, the days
when there were still pike and muskie in the river),
and Rosemary, who had been her pupil – she
was mangled so thoroughly by the car, we left
the casket closed. Around it some hushed boys
in blue school jackets recalled the dusk they watched her
swimming naked, till she looked up and saw
the red points of their cigarettes in the bushes,
and realized, and ran. In the next room the factions
of the Harrises each faced their no-man's-land,
the aisle through the folding chairs. Two infirm brothers
still hate the widow of the brother killed in the war –
she sided with their father when he fought them
to take back the company: fires and civic improvements
have destroyed or covered up all the bricks it laid.

They have to be free for this. So I compose
the limbs, pipe in the music, and light and scent
a blond chapel. The sonatas in the background
are likewise composed, corpses of some idea
as this house is and the brick church across the street.
But my work is always quickly taken away
to enrich the ground of the memorial park –
a better place than any the children are given
in this rusting, cracking town. Its high brick wall,
ivy-covered, shuts out the surrounding streets
of packed identical houses, its gate closes

against pool halls and wholesale textile shops.
Inside, trees tower as they should
over toy marble buildings and carved inscriptions:
names, years, and loves. And privileged beings,
mere motions, dart in imagination
among squirrels and crowds of finches feeding
and flickering, between porticoes and long stairs
in a green city without sewers or corrupt parties.
Sounds of the other city, horns, a lawnmower droning,
come from far off to fall asleep in this
decorum, this order.

                        Because an order must
be imposed on human corpses. Only beings that are light
and small leave bodies possessed of their own grace.
Once I saw a fragile turquoise wing
fallen among wood chips and pine cones:
the thaw had uncovered it beside a headstone
in greening spring grass, and it was still as soft
as a loved cheek. Far different is the massive
rot of large animals that die untended:
a horse bloating in a flood's yellow silt,
an aged cow fallen dead by a mustard tree –
and the toothless, reptile-skinned old woman who tripped
one night, drunk, into a window well
two stories deep behind an empty warehouse
and lay there days unnoticed among flies and mice.
I washed and drained the lightly nibbled flesh
that no one claimed, that the morgue attendants brought
to my house: the city provides for this.
I composed her limbs and we put her with the rest.

My feet were floating away from me. Already
they were so far I could no longer feel them.
But I despised them, and didn't trouble about it.

My wife screamed and screamed at me as the feet
drifted beyond her. She tried to wake me, shouting,
Why don't you bring them back?

The doctor wanted to tie them down. He wanted
to save them by cutting pieces off: by doling them,
bite by bite, to the ground, he thought he could delay

their disappearance. And he was right, no doubt.
But I didn't want it. Nor did I want too great a haste
in my falling apart, no spectacular decay:

nothing so opulent. Just something small, even
petty: to be, unknown to myself, each day
a little faster, without wanting it, dying out.

Now
no thing is pure
but the senses
still
create and taste
of all things
the purity.

The eye in bright poisoned air, the tongue
drowning itself for joy in water white
from gleaming faucets,
          pure silver
          reflecting in miniature
          spring windows,
          a vase of forsythia on a sill ...
the tongue and eye
taste purity.

Then memory brings its knowledge
and the words of trustworthy witnesses,
the ones who have delved, who have gone there
where nothing is sense:
          cancerous infusions, intangible as spirit,
          from waving fields, mighty mills,
          sublime images of peace and power,
and unknowable
chemicals sent to eat chemicals
by the guardians, desperately tired.

Till all the being abhors and savours
the pure world it creates, the pure delight
the senses take in ignorance,
and wonders at itself:
I walk in a death I don't know.
I revel in the body of this death.

In Mexico the beef is tough:
the people there let the cows wander around
and they grow strong, struggling up red mountains
and along dead rivers
between clumps of grass as far-flung as desert wells.

Human jaws must work hard to chew that beef.
Afterwards in hotel rooms
a sense of wakeful eagerness remains,
a sense of grateful weariness, of disengagement and of waiting,
in the joint of the tired jaws and the throat muscles,
and a sense of open space between the teeth.

Your lover has visited Mexico.
What now, you sweet dissolving steaks of Illinois?
Surely the prodigal will come back to you.
Surely again forgetfulness will sink
the mouth of the cowboy deep
in the soft rump
of his chained and pampered queen.

His flag-shrouded coffin let down from the sky
by a powerful machine. The flag-shroud,
red and white, blood and blank: the rivers
made straight under the beauty of a night sky
revised from profusion to fifty stars
in ordered commerce. Thump of cannon,
concussive wing-beat of invisible doves
over his cradle, in Yorba Linda's air
that is not air so much as brilliance, pure freshness,
and peace, an ecstasy yet a conservation: stillness that knows
to disturb nothing unless there is dire need.

Now's my time to put on muffled memories
of ancient eloquence – 'All in all,
I shall not see his like again' – as a suit
that fits badly, just like the common man's,
yet is made of cloth so expensive it strikes awe.
For he was one who climbed to the stars
but never forgot his home. It would be foolish here
to raise again the old squabble over the corpses
of heroes: do they act with will and power
or only as helpless ciphers of what happens?
Did the rage for peace burning in our streets
drive him out of the war?
Was it our valedictory, his and mine, expressive
of our true love, when we poured fire on Cambodia
and released through cracks in the burnt ground
a demon of pure hatred for all things human?
Forbidden by our people to fight another people,
at least we killed until the last moment possible
and so punished both enemies. No question:
praise him as one who never gave up: this much
is undeniable, and admired by all.

And yet our enemies too never gave up.
Standing here out of power I can see them well:
how his indomitable virtue has been made
into a pattern, a method all can buy,

sold on television: tapes
that will imprint it on brains as they go driving
back and forth on the Santa Monica all day.
A perfect machine: whatever stupidity or crime
humans commit, now they know how to proclaim it
blandly, fiercely, never wavering,
to the very end of their lives
and beyond. They pass it down to others:
each vice and triviality becomes a tradition
maintained by the most pious conservatism,
and gives back to its adherents the gift
of being insolent and invulnerable.
Richard, powerful king: I seem to see him
crucified on his own strength, crucified forever
as charlatans tell that his example taught them,
though only primitively, how to bond error
with self-righteousness and mechanical technique.

Better to remember what is fact: his promise
the war would end, and when he was driven from power
it was over. I must clear my mind and speak
the thoughts I have laid out: just now some other mind
was whispering in me. It's as if I had been the mate
of a great captain, but then I saw that we two
were only fragments of someone else's thought.
For a moment I glimpsed an idea we belong to.
And we were jostled by all its other fragments.
Suddenly the pair of us no longer were lone hunters
of the whale-fish. Now we heard the deep intentions
of the whale-people, saw their couplings, the love
of male and female, parent and child; we felt
the divine mercy and indifference of ocean
surrounding and filling them. Also the shores
were with us, because that mind was thinking
at once of our ship and us and the far away
white wooden ports between forest and sea, the waving
women, God's word in the chapel, Jonah, Ishmael,
the outcast on the salt or naphtha deserts

sinking into sand or walking the waves. Was thinking
equally of people from every land, golden and red
and black, and so their power also crossed my mind
and seemed to lie in my bed with arms around me,
in chanted poems and prayers, in spears,
intricate carvings and tattoos.

And then I kicked hard and suddenly was fleeing
through the country's dark interior
on a huge black horse named Credulity.
With one stride he bounded from Washington and New York
to a vile slum on the mountain above Wheeling
and the Ohio. Next like a tornado he knocked down
a town of huts and trailers in Oklahoma.
At his third step he was caught and penned in barbed wire
with other scabbed mustangs on a dusty weedless lot
outside Cheyenne. At every place, squat people
were shouting, 'Wield us,' and they waved their flag:
the same one he is wrapped in. The fourth step
I took myself. I came to Yorba Linda
to watch the helicopter bring his coffin,
to praise him as the all-comprehending one,
who alone knew the secret meanings of 'wealth' and 'peace,'
who bore in his own body all we had done
and all we hoped for, and to let my visions cease.

ON A LINE BY CATULLUS

I love and I hate:
is there more than that?
A perfect summary
of what we must repeat,
that it's all one,
joy and pain.
And I suspect the joy –
it may be only
boredom exalting
its own body.
But I love the fact
that I suffer
and suffer the fact
that I love.
And festoon this stodgy
total significance
in plumes of poetry,
that the apparent
bright birds flying up
new and original
must ingeniously
be plucked ever
to reveal
at all –
and then only dimly –
the one and never
changing anatomy.

ON DISTINCTION

We won't pretend we're not hungry for distinction
but what can ever distinguish us enough?
This country, this language won't last long, the race
will die, later the cockroach, earth itself,

and last this beer bottle: silicon fused by man,
almost indestructible, like a soul:
it will go spinning ever farther from the nearest thing
until space, continually deepening, drowns in itself.

Yet we keep a hungry eye on old schoolmates
and everyone born in the year of our own birth,
and spend the nights in ranting over them,
their money, fashionable companions, pliant critics.

To live just a little longer than they do:
that would be triumph. Hence exercise and diets,
and the squabble over who will write the history
of this paradise of demons casting each other out.

A FORMER STUDENT

I am the tutor of a perished king,
a suicide.
I taught him how to triumph but he died.

From a high rock in his serrated thought,
tempted, he leapt
on desert, city, empire, as they slept.

What was my rule of life? That he should hold
himself apart?
Or excel everywhere by strength and art?

The outward man in bright accomplishment
gives sign of blessing.
Yet he who shuns all wealth knows strength unceasing.

Poor prince – contemptuous ghost inferior
to those he scorns –
some nights in lightless streets where the foghorns

rattle the windows, harry papers and cans,
I meet him still
seeking a beauty to erect his will.

Humid and thin in the unbearable summer,
this spirit creeps
once again through the flesh where its youth sleeps.

O buono Appollo, a l'ultima lavoro
fammi del tuo valor sì fatto vaso,
come dimandi a dar l'amato alloro....
Entra nel petto mio, e spira tue
sì come quando Marsïa traesti
de la vagina de le membra sue.
– *Paradiso* I. 13–15, 19–21

Although they have their stories of creation
ripped from the womb of the male god's male wife,
or of this world as the one daughter of a virgin,

it is hard to convey to the most primitive peoples
the idea of sexual inversion. And
if it can be made clear to them, they laugh.

Such is the opinion of those whose life is food,
women who dive in frigid water collecting shellfish,
men who cut and sharpen sticks,

the people who shelter in twig lean-tos and pray
to Father Elephant not to crush them too often,
the people who know how to gather and sustain

fire but not how to make it,
who multiply and dwindle by the mystery
of the dwindling or multiplication of the herds,

whose neighbours have driven them into the least
desirable lands, the desert, ice, or deep forest,
who live by the ocean but never venture on it,

paint the eland on the rock and dance the dance
of thrusting the great snake once more back into the pit,
and sing to the stars, those great hunters following

a wounded beast over the horizon, to return.
In the evolution of song, these people live

in an era before the coming of Apollo,

who brought, it is said, inversion down from heaven.
Once there was Marsyas, great human singer
of whom nothing now is known, and musical Apollo

first appeared on the earth in jealous anger
and peeled the skin whole from Marsyas' body,
turning it inside out, savouring the unmelodious agony

of the master's screaming and clumsy death-rattle.
Then he turned and bestowed the gift, his love,
upon Olympos, Marsyas' young disciple,

who had stood by, gaping. Afterwards the boy,
having played for years the two flutes of Apollo,
that of illusory flesh and that of heavenly silver,

was converted to new music and forgot the old.
There exists, from the time of the rebirth of learning,
a work that shows Apollonian knowledge returning

after a dark age without medicine, philosophic song,
or law ... after an age of many deaths
but by swords and maces, not the golden bow.

It is a drawing in which the naked god
dandles a naked youth astride of his left knee:
Olympos no doubt. A woman, foreground right,

looks on with jealous grief and rage
in isolated profile – and how inelegant
is the fleshy, hanging distension of womb and buttocks,

how fine by comparison the curve of the god's index
just touching the young man's thin limp pizzle
in a gesture of creation;

how light, next to the turgid female,
the pair's mild expressions, amusement, confused abandon.
Within this drawing the artist has left a puzzle:

on a withered fingerlike branch beside the artist-god
hangs something empty – maybe a chiton flung aside,
maybe the pelt of Marsyas. Who can decide?

There's not enough information in the picture.
But there is someone who has solved the mystery,
and sings again to be the continuance

of forgotten Marsyas, though of that murdered joy
there remains only defiance: that everything is wrong,
men and men, men and women, and the gods,

and this is the only content of true song.

Thirty years he sat on the dark ground,
his back against the wall that sheltered the harsh table.
An infantile spear of grass towered up between his spread legs,
its open face before his face, one-featured, overshadowing:
bland smile as of a knife edge, green in dripping renewal,
one more among the endless spears in their ranks
repeated out of sight, beyond fallen mills and mounds of slag
to the meadow's forest wall, and past the smoke hills.
Perfume rose from its groin in the mud,
a dark ring where the stem leapt from the root:
it seemed to him the storm's source, and humiliation
when lightning rolled along a glistening brick wall,
and concrete's dust was laid and polished, flashing.
Then the hoarse shouts at the table were drowned as water
was renewed in him, rising, pouring down, covering his sides,
the elm's curved gracious fork, and the pure iron chimney.

The mysterious crane of her left arm
                                    pivoting,
the block and tackle rippling
                                    its supple housing,
and in her eye as in a snake's or rabbit's
the obvious, hungry calculation.
                                    And beneath:
the useless mouldings of her breasts, the forms
and the fillips:
                    like decorations made
                        by an innocent artisan
who once was here
        and prayed
            and remembered Pan
                    in smoke blown from the smelters.

At night on the watery road,
a white deserted trail glimmering beside the stream,
he would stop the starved weaver, the demobbed soldier,
as they hobbled mumbling.

There are still signs of him: he placed
acanthus on boiler doors,
        grapes and great stone heads on the cornices of banks,
            he asked the beggar for his story
and took him to lodge at least one night at a cottage
        that shone above unscrolled water
            sparkling in its sleep.

Secure now in the river's and the beggar's
sheltered peace,
                he wandered again
back into the deceiving, divulging night,
considering that he knew good
                    of the not-human.

And she: random and exquisite,
the thin beauty tacked across those pumps, her breasts,

for a while blinded me to everything.
For a while it was pleasure
                    though I don't forget
why the stars this evening
        appeared to leap from the sea
                    over the horizon of her belly
breathing on the sand (hers
                    is the shape
that water longs for
in all its shapes and its caressing,
                    its howling
changes). Though I still stumble
in the poor fallen night
                    until the sun
appears, because the earth rolls forward,
and this scrap where we are lying plunges down
beneath the constant fire. I
        like all
            seeing the dawn
                can't help
                    but say,
'It rises.'

        And winter too
will seem brilliant, when it comes,
        because she loves it:
            with the artisan's love of rest,
            which winter commands: the locked season, of pure
colours and forms burning and secluded
        in candid outline, of the forced need to live
            sheltered, close to the fire,
on the hoarded produce of dead summer
and once-triumphant arms.

            I saw her
loving, more than sunrise,
winter and hope because her will
is a machine of that sort which works

on whatever is left – even if it longs
       and cries out with antiquated gears
           to stop, it goes on working because
               the parts were thrown together
     to work
until the end.

But the light of this explanation
went out. And in the dark again there was
nothing
       but what the eye sees:
the endless, the starving, the prolific,
ignorance hived in winter,
     her at the heart of the gaze
         and the needful power to love her.

My disciples said to the space where I had been,
'No one knows your thoughts, Master. Your book
and the scents of night betray nothing to the black air.'

But it was not the space where I had been.
The false legend had betrayed them. The disaster
of age had overtaken me entirely elsewhere.

Nothing but their mistaken, rash imagination
in that pleasant shrine might by ignorance be made
the ghost and silence they think I'm armoured in.

But let me say this, now, to those song-forsaken
lovers of mine, say one thing clear and loud.
In every poem – take that of this cricket pausing

between two shrills – which scholars claim is lost
(though it's well known, it simply has no words),
I mean each sound for rending and revelation.

The lines ran on. In the evenings that befell our country in those
  days
they grew more visible, as vapour trails turn rose-red when the
  sun falls under them.

These lines cut straight across a great perfect plane decorated
  here and there with trompe l'oeil
forested hills, snowy mountains, butte- and canyon-carving winds
  and rivers.

They made a vast diagram in relief spread out on the ground. But
  on what ground?
No one knew of anyone who had seen the ground. In some of the
  lines that night

heads twisted over shoulders and whispered voices discussed this
  fact.
Or rather, they shouted histrionically, pretending to whisper,
  because they wanted to cry out

but only whispers were allowed. Especially by proud aspirants to
  humility
who composed the rarest lines: those that stretched out to
  pathetic thinness, only sparse member points

defining vectors across gold space: lines of big moneymakers and
  somewhat thicker
lines of little moneymakers, lined up to scam or be scammed,
  waiting all night.

And maybe as they whispered they were the lucky ones, because
  their lines,
less populated, gave each point the luxury of some space along its
  own direction.

It was only where these lines were always crossed everywhere by
  all the others at all angles
that they were jammed, sweated, stomped, stunk, beshat, shot,

jostled, crowded, stripped, and eaten.

Complaining bitterly yet content, whistling a tuneless tune, they
    would shoulder their bite-bladed
broad-axes, factory-made shells, procedural precision, dull
    volatile lunacy with available leisure,

and stride off happy to their work in long chains, in a sort of
    plot,
into a sort of damp brick basement without sanitary facilities
    they never leave.

And the new darkness turned up other apocalypses of loosely
    fitting ever repeating parts:
resurrected bloodlines a thousand names long, Friday night car and
    girl lines,

lines of beggars along the rows of shopfronts, and two lines of
    passersby:
the one that walks close to the beggars, each person dropping a
    coin into each cup,

until, having no further coins, the people in this line push and
    fight in
among the beggars, sit down against the walls and project their
    hands;

and the other, far from beggars and givers alike, composed of
    people passing
quickly, following each other to add themselves to more deeply
    desired columns:

a purposeful line, but disturbed by muddy tributaries – lines of
    party-leavers laughing
like a file of hyenas cameoed against a red rising moon on the
    crest of a low ridge.

Lines of the genitally obstructed, the emotionally disturbed, the

ones who've crumbled
before the length of lines, retreating wall-eyed into doorless
    alcoves.

Long lines of print failing to mention the failure of the long
    line of thinkers
who overcame the subject-object, mind-brain, spirit-body split:
    for, banished,

it reemerged at once in the form of a line of mumbling shouting
    dribblers
who creak out 'Spare some change' like gears out of alignment,
    queued up

on the sidewalks, one per block, all the way to the gates of the
    asylum,
where the corridors, cells, latrines, mess halls, wards, and
    grounds are covered with patient lines.

And is a line a line to one who refuses to know that it exists and
    he or she is in it,
even though it surely does to the million scholars lined up at
    publishers' doors with manuscripts on this question?

And does the line that exists in the world but not in the mind
    fail in fact to exist?
Are only bitter realists aligned, unable ever to forget the lines
    of their argument?

So poets rise up again, because now once more humans are moved to
    write the praise of folly –
that there is god and no lines if you believe, lines and no god if
    you will only know what's real –

and struck by this intuition, each one, certain he is the first,
    composes all night in rolling frenzy,
and in the morning, rushing to the agora, discovers endless lines
    there

of new poets filling the streets to the city centre from every
    direction,
all waving their divine odes, and lines up at the end of a line,
    waving his divine ode.

In fact, though, each poem, each poet, is unique, incomparable, a
    world unto itself,
and the bindings of books delineating minute differences run down
    a billion shelves,

till the eye hates itself that there is another eye, the hand that
    there is another hand,
and the buttocks hate the anus, testes the penis, breasts and
    ovaries the canal, lips the tongue, lungs the heart.

Ignored for endless ages, now suddenly the most loved and most
    despised
of all public figures, the prophets of the line came forward in
    long procession,

each in desiringly gentle voice over loudspeakers teaching the
    queues how to live
the dissolving volumes of their democracy. In a million different
    voices

they prayed in unison that everyone should ignore them, the
    prophets,
and be, each person, unprecedented, strange and unestranged, self-
    created.

Each was to be superior to all. And the lines took this to heart,
    all chanting together,
'Ignore me and be unprecedented, strange and unestranged, self-
    created.'

Sometimes when they were chanting and the lines of fires in the
    night – trash fires, building fires –
flickered almost dead, the lines seemed to merge, as if there were

only one,

a line at a door, of people needing to get whatever might be about
   to be handed out.
And you couldn't see if the door was open and the feet were
   shuffling slowly in

or if it was closed somewhere far up ahead, and the line was
   stopped as always.
One thing you could see: now that there was nowhere else, people
   were making a life of the line,

adapting what they knew. If a man lined up in front of a woman, he
   wanted to be behind
to use or service her. If behind, he wanted to be in front, to
   drag her, as owner or dray.

And they found praises for the line, as follows: 'It revels in
   tests and sport;
it draws distinctions between before and after, when in the middle
   of the line

the door out of nowhere closes like a blade, parting those who
   have made it through
from those at the back, and sometimes cutting a single body in
   half.

Though inarticulate, the line worships the door, whether closed
   and breaking
the line as it shoves forward, or still open till who knows when,
   like a jaw.

Though the line has no front or end, though there is no heaven or
   hell,
where the jaw-door snaps, that point is always the centre, and
   then there is inside and out.'

Now cheers, hats, batons, trumpet-blasts, starburst rockets,

balloons, and smoke
rise up along all the lines, which intersect in not quite
    infinitely intricate square patterns,

and girl machines fill every avenue, rows of bare thighs flashing
    and spicily wrapped breasts,
even more than on this late summer night come down the conveyors
    of the chicken factories.

In each of the deserted sidestreets along the route of the
    celebration
one melancholic walks, pursuing a line of thought, unwittingly
    parallel to all his confreres,

while in each of the deserted towers lining the grand boulevards,
    one mad assassin
tries to line up his sights on one of the presidents leading one
    of the parades.

Seen from such high vantage, the lines – black or white hair,
    sunburnt bald crowns,
feathers, scarves, and baseball caps – cut through the placid cubed
    white city like arroyos

in a land ruined long ago by a fury of rushing water, seemingly
    never to end,
and afterwards preserved forever unchanging by the still greater
    power of drought.

Why was that city there in the middle of my sleep?

Decaying in the deeply forested virgin plains of sleep, grey-green and golden wet, with paths that wander a long time beside streams before they turn to cross the silver water: from fresh, unsettled tracts of sleep rose that narrow squalid city, ancient in its strip of slag.

Its women kneaded a chalky dough, the same their flesh seemed made of. As they went through streets twisted between brick hives, rattling on the walls, stale crumbs rattling on their tin dishes, they knew but could not hear the far-off tramp of men and children into high corroded metal doors or rocky holes: a million feet in such unison, they were one pair of feet, one worker all alone.

There in the flowering desert it stood still labouring: the city where we were born, the city we buried long ago. No dream but the opposite: a moment of pure waking. Helpless between sleep's two ranges – the one that wells up from yesterday's dark, the other that sinks toward dawn – I saw it with all its people, for no reason, not wanting to.

No matter that they had escaped already into death and forgottenness: now it would never let them go. So they went on working where the mines had collapsed long since, the mills rotted. Just as before, the wavering tapping of their hands each day wore down the rock more than an era of rain.

Then watching, I fell back unaware to sleep – sleep with blue and dark-gold meadows, with wheeling crowds of silent birds but no ploughed field, no houses, ruins, tools of the pioneer – and moving out through fresh woods I left behind that city and people who had to die, work, and be.

There is a wren house invisible now because, as people say,
it's destroyed long ago and vanished: wooden on a wooden pole,
head-high to a grown man as if the homemade house, with wrens
going and coming in their roughly sawn round doors or stopping
to rest on a grainy threshold, is another human face
to look him in the eye and talk. But it's much taller to
a child: up past my farthest reaches the excited wrens
rush all day between their house, the peach tree, and bright vines
sheltering my grandmother's rough red wall – rough dusky red
because it's made with paving brick, not light smooth building
     brick,
my grandmother invisible too, being as people call it dead.

Both houses hers, one for the wrens rent free to rhyme their song
of fresh syllables: 'Find its central moment and the day
is yours.' Now's February, as it was the time she died
and as she died I had to stay – I thought – here in this city,
and be too busy to think of her, preserving my pathetic
job, licking up my substance by writing a lying report
to get some government money for a businessman. But I
do not, for this, see Toronto as a pit like those where now
the Roman slaves dig salt, no light or hope, and no one troubles
himself about their rescue, saying they all died and ended
ages ago and can't be helped or charged now against me.

Wrong, say the wrens, and wrench me back to life. Once I stood
on the asphalt height of the parking lot behind the Church
of the Transfiguration, reciting her favourite prayer to the moon
over the banks and CN Tower, to return her to her garden,
remembering what she told me from her bed after the stroke
at the foot of the cellar stairs: I prayed to all the saints in
     heaven
and no one heard me. Me neither. What I asked for didn't happen.
But what I wanted? A wren is a mighty being, but to sing
my wants is maybe beyond even him. Whatever can
be destroyed is going to be destroyed. Patience, patience.
Hate what needs to be hated. All is finished. All's completed.

ACKNOWLEDGEMENTS & THANKS

The author thanks the Canada Council, and the following
periodicals, in which the poems in this book previously
appeared: *The Alembic, The American Literary Review, The
Antigonish Review, ARC, Borderlands, Canadian Literature,
Commonweal, The Dalhousie Review, Descant, Event, The
Fiddlehead, 52 Pickup 76, The Hudson Review, El Huevo
Filosófico, The Journal, The Malahat Review, Matrix, The Paris
Review, The Partisan Review, Quarry, Queen's Quarterly,
Poetry Canada, The Spoon River Poetry Review,* and *The Yale
Review.* 'Artisan and Clerk' was reprinted (from *The Yale
Review*) in *The Best American Poetry 1998,* ed. John Hollander
(New York: Charles Scribners' Sons, 1998); that poem and ten of
the others were reprinted in the chapbook *Twelve Poems*
(Toronto: Micro Prose, 1997). 'On Distinction' was reprinted
(from *The Antigonish Review*) in *Anthology of Magazine Verse
and Yearbook of American Poetry 1995–96,* ed. Alan F. Pater
(Beverly Hills: Monitor Book Co., 1997). 'The Little Walls Before
China,' nominated by *Event,* was a finalist for the 1997 National
Magazine Award in poetry. A few of the poems have also
appeared in Spanish translations by Gilberto Meza in my book
Ciudad interior (Zacatecas, Mexico: Universidad Autónoma de
Zacatecas, 1993).

Thanks for help in revising many of these poems and the book
as a whole to Theresa Moritz, John Donlan, Don McKay, and Jan
Zwicky who edited the final version for Brick Books; and to John
Reibetanz for his decisive advice not only on many of these
poems but on my previous books *Mahoning* and *A Houseboat
on the Styx.*

Manifestation, l. 24:
Artaud died of rectal cancer.

Science of Limits, final line:
Allusion to the famous poem by Aimé Césaire.

The Little Walls Before China:
Ch'in Shih-huang-ti, the ruler from whom the word China
comes, initiated the Great Wall, incorporating or replacing the
many small walls which were a feature of the defence strategy of
local states. It was Shih (Ch'in is his dynasty's name, huang-ti
means 'first emperor') who took the initial steps to create the
unified Chinese empire about 246 BC.

Rest on the Flight into Egypt:
The painting of this traditional subject which the poem refers to
is in the Art Gallery of Ontario. There is not, in fact, a postcard
of it.

Landscape:
The first line quotes George Dillon's translation of the first line
of Baudelaire's 'Paysage' (*Flowers of Evil*, trans. George Dillon
and Edna St. Vincent Millay, 1936).

That Day, l. 15:
Hamlet IV. vii., Gertrude speaking of Ophelia's drowning: 'There
with fantastic garlands did she come/Of cornflowers, nettles,
daisies, and long purples,/That liberal shepherds give a grosser
name,/But our cold maids do dead men's fingers call them.'

The Undertaker:
The epigraph, from César Vallejo's 'Los Desgraciados,' means
'You have to eat, but, I tell myself, don't grieve, because grief
and sobbing beside the tomb are not for the poor.'

Kissinger at the Funeral of Nixon:
For President Nixon's ceremonial funeral, his catafalque, the
casket draped in a large United States flag, was brought by
military helicopter to his estate at Yorba Linda, California, and
was lowered to the ground before the assembled dignitaries and
mourners.

Ode to Apollo:
The epigraph means 'O good Apollo, make me such a fit vessel
of your power as you require, worthy of being given your
beloved laurel.... Come, breathe into my breast, just as you did
when you pulled Marsyas out of the sheath of his members.'
Stanza two paraphrases observations of Bronislaw Malinowski:
cf. *Sex and Repression in Savage Society* (1927; rpt. 1955), pp.
86–7; also *The Sexual Life of Savages in North-Western
Melanesia* (1929; third ed. 1932; rpt. 1957), p. 370; also pp.
396–99. The myth of the music contest between Apollo and
Marsyas (originator of the flute and, in some versions, originator
rather than Pan of the syrinx or pan flute), with the subsequent
flaying of Marsyas by Apollo, embodied the ancient theme of the
enmity between the lyre and the flute. Olympos is mentioned in
classical sources as a musical apprentice of Marsyas. In the
Renaissance this story often was used to allegorize the
punishment of pride; divine art and inspiration versus low art;
the revelation of truth or virtue hidden beneath error and
ugliness; or the triumph of *harmonia*, of the political or cosmic
order, over revolution and evil. I have purposely 'mistaken' the
myth in various ways, chiefly by reversing the polarity of
honour between the two main characters, and by making Apollo
take over, for his own purposes, the flute. The artwork described
in stanzas 13–20 is closely based on a Renaissance drawing I
once saw in an art book but did not make a note of and now
cannot trace.

A. F. Moritz has published two previous books with Brick, *Song of Fear* (1992) and *Mahoning* (1994). His most recent books are *A Houseboat on the Styx* (1998), a long poem, and two translations in collaboration with his wife, Theresa Moritz, from the work of Ludwig Zeller: *Body of Insomnia* (1996), poems, and *Rio Loa: Station of Dreams* (1999), a novel. Moritz's poetry has received honours including the Award in Literature of the American Academy and Institute of Arts and Letters, a Guggenheim Foundation fellowship, an Ingram Merrill Foundation fellowship, and selection to the Princeton Series of Contemporary Poets. Other collections of his poems are *Here* (1975), *Black Orchid* (1981), *The Visitation* (1983), *The Tradition* (1986), *The Ruined Cottage* (1993), and *Phantoms in the Ark* (1994). He has lived since 1974 in Toronto, where he works as a writer and as a lecturer at the University of Toronto.